Throughline

poems by

Cora McCann Liderbach

Finishing Line Press
Georgetown, Kentucky

Throughline

*To Mark, for your steadfast love & support,
and to friends of Lois everywhere*

Copyright © 2024 by Cora McCann Liderbach
ISBN 979-8-88838-747-4 First Edition
All rights reserved under International and Pan-American Copyright Conventions. No part of this book may be reproduced in any manner whatsoever without written permission from the publisher, except in the case of brief quotations embodied in critical articles and reviews.

ACKNOWLEDGMENTS

Ariel's Dream Journal: "Becalmed"
Ariel's Dream digital: "Peace Amid the Pandemic"
Crab Creek Review: "Wings"
Grand Little Things: "Premonition"
Hole in the Head Review: "Walt Whitman, Ray Bradbury and Me"
Last Stanza Poetry Journal: "Poem for the Departed"
Light Enters the Grove, a poetic inventory of Cuyahoga Valley National Park, Kent State University Wick Poetry Center: "Nothing Common About This Dandelion"
Luna Negra Magazine: "Punchline"
OpenDoor Magazine: "Bessie;" "Still, Still, Still"
Poem for Cleveland anthology: "Abecedarian Weather, Cleveland, Ohio," "Ode to Lakewood"
Quiet Diamonds: "Reasons to Celebrate," "Holding Pattern: 2020"
The RavensPerch: "Word Pictures," "A High Capacity for Suffering," "Raft"

Publisher: Leah Huete de Maines
Editor: Christen Kincaid
Cover Art: Sara Liderbach Williams
Author Photo: Dale Omori
Cover Design: Elizabeth Maines McCleavy

Order online: www.finishinglinepress.com
also available on amazon.com

Author inquiries and mail orders:
Finishing Line Press
PO Box 1626
Georgetown, Kentucky 40324
USA

Contents

Word Pictures 1
Wings 2
Bessie 3
Punchline 4
The Cowrie Shell 5
Raft 6
Shaky 7
when the bottom dropped out 9
Sign on a Country Road 10
Premonition 11
A Poet Awaits Deep Brain Stimulation 12
Reasons to Celebrate 13
A High Capacity for Suffering 14
Still, Still, Still 16
Holding Pattern: 2020 17
Becalmed 18
Peace Amid the Pandemic 19
Nothing Common About This Dandelion 20
suitcase 21
Thirteen Ways of Looking at a Lake 22
Throughline 24
Today: What's Beautiful 25
requiem for a nightmare 27
Abecedarian Weather, Cleveland, Ohio 28
Walt Whitman, Ray Bradbury and Me 30
Ode to Lakewood, Ohio 31
Erie Pantoum 32
Poetry, after Pablo Neruda 33

Word Pictures

She came from a family of fast talkers, but her mind moved faster than her tongue. She was quick to the heart of a matter, quick to sympathize, quick to draw conclusions but quicker to draw, pencil scratching faster than words could form. She thought in cartoons, in word balloons; words slowed as they left her mouth, arrived late, fell into conversations out of sync. She misspoke, miscued, forgot punchlines, missed the boat, missed the harbor more. Spent years searching her purpose, college, marriage, family, writing, hundreds, thousands, millions of words, newsletters, blogs, brochures—till words began to billow out in pictures, render sunsets in pastel, cloud banks in charcoal, etch sadness and hope onto shorelines in ink.

Wings

The robin flies low over snowy yards, lands in the road
and, cocking its head the way robins do, searches
for worms. It's the kind of day—44 degrees, drizzle

rippling rings in puddles, sky blending with snow
smudged by exhaust—that keeps most humans nesting
in armchairs by the window. But a robin's got to eat

and the doctor says you've got to walk. Leaves pale
as postal wrap cling to alders; a string of plastic
berries festoons a small pine. Desiccated hydrangeas

punctuate rain-blackened trees. A southwest wind
weaves the topmost branches of an oak through the sky's
loom. And now a robin who's no longer

a robin sits at the tarmac's edge, motionless ball
of feathers and fluff, beak open, eye shut. You watch one
futile wing waft up, a burst of orange—a salute

to passing brilliance—and pray that your own
fledgling, winging unknown skies after countless false
starts, meets mercy wherever he lands.

Bessie

       Sunset fades to indigo above the shoreline's
       fairy lights / Lake Erie's frigid waters murmur

you're here now, you're here / waves relax you, invite the
imagination to roam / plumb the murky depths / in your mind's

          eye, you spot her / long, reptilian body slithering
          on silt / eyes large, sleepy, watchful over

      triple rows of teeth / fins rotating slightly / tail trailing /
      but the Lake Erie Monster is shy / doesn't like attention

        passing sailors fired muskets on her / labeled her
        vicious / likened her to a sturgeon, the ugliest

beast in the Great Lakes / Bessie has tired of the outlandish
fiction / lived for three centuries / her heavy body

          dredging the lake floor / hasn't she earned the right
          to peace in home waters? / to pause, as you do

             now / to watch
             the moon mount

                 a sapphire dome?

Punchline

He was just a Jersey boy,
a wisecracker, a wit; too
nearsighted for stickball.
Hungry for history and art,
schooled by example.
And if he later forgot
to teach kindness or patience—
he could only parrot
what he learned from his mother
and the nuns at St. Aloysius.
And if he held too fast to fear—
it was merely the memory
of onion sandwiches
in the Great Depression
lingering. And if he preferred
evenings at Jimmy O'Neil's
to evenings at home—it was
because his quiet father showed
him the comfort of distance
from discord—and the warmth
a tumbler of whiskey
and a punchline, well-landed,
could bring.

The Cowrie Shell

The prize from my beach vacation
glowed with leopard spots

on my childhood window sill,
perfect, unbroken.

My fingers loved its round,
gleaming smoothness.

After several days, a waft
of decay wound through

the room I shared with my sister.
How we laughed when I traced

the foul smell to the corpse
inside my precious find

and threw it in the trash.
Looking back, I think

of the poor creature I kidnapped,
who'd never again prowl
the sea floor,

powered by a solo foot,
licking algae from rocks

for breakfast.

Raft

I want to float downriver in a raft of otters—
belly up, pup nestled on my tummy
or wrapped in seaweed as I hunt
for lunch—hold a small, sleek
paw in mine and nap the day
away, our thick pelts
protection against
the wet of river.

I want to be an otter in my next life—
odd since I'm a loner in this one,
poets tend to be—but something
about the way otters slither
and slide over one
another, romping
and wrestling,
hanging

in twos, threes and fours, their lodge
spanning a stream, reminds me
of what we missed—ten kids
adrift in childhood seas,
unmoored,
riding
solo.

Shaky

Why are you shaking? For thirty years
I can't answer, know only that I shake

      like my mom, who shakes like her mom,
      who shakes like her dad. Unaware

a temblor jars our family tree,
judders genes from Swedish forebears

      into my branch. Brain miscues muscles
      to battle over direction, intention. I hear

You're shivering, you must be cold
when I'm warm, *You're saying no?*

      when I mean yes. Agitating adolescence,
      anxiety and audiences amplify jitters

when I raise chalk to blackboard, glass
of water on a date, sign for my first

      driver's license, cop objecting,
      You're gonna need a doctor's exam.

I assume it's weakness, some
compulsion to mimic my mother,

      never meet anyone young like me
      reeling from these aftershocks, hands,

head, voice dancing. My dreams—art,
music—shift like tectonic plates

      to writing as fingers fumble over canvas
      and fret, find purchase on a keyboard.

Doctors finally name the seism *essential
tremor,* say alcohol quiets the quaking,

> *Glad you work, lots of folks are drunks
> who never leave the house,* prescribe

medicines, injections that can't withstand
the unsteadiness of age. But time is kind,

> teaches me to care less what others
> think, to chuckle at mishaps, open

my guarded heart, allow a poem to knit
together the fractured fault lines

> of my life, swallow another evening
> whole on my laptop at two a.m.

when the bottom dropped out

you missed signs along the way, they said / mistook affection for devotion / charm for connection / buried your ache in the sand like something precious / ties unraveling, gut protesting (funny how the body knows) / suddenly awash in grief / aswirl in a sea change of someone else's choosing / tumbling in waves of regret / gulping saltwater / yet the earth's own star kept shining / settled the swells / breached the nimbus clouds enfolding you / warmed your dripping skin / lit the shoal beneath your feet / so you stood and straightened / crossed the strand / pound of surf fading in your ears / eyes ever watchful / for signs

Sign on a Country Road

We pitched our tent by the swamp
where the big catfish got away from you,
a place you found beautiful, otherworldly.

I saw waterlogged trees the color of bone,
stagnation and death, but felt newly alive.
You slipped a night crawler on a hook,

sunk the line into darkness. Where I
imagined mere rot and muck, you saw
a wily, whiskered catfish just waiting

for you. We caught nothing worth
keeping, so you took my hand to stroll
the sunbaked road—no traffic,

dog or two barking by post-mounted
mailboxes—when the sign on one
stopped us short—Mark & Cora,

it read, Roofing—our names in startling
conjunction, hinting the future.
We packed up the orange tent

and drove your rusty Toyota back
to the city, where streetlights bathed
our pillows as we struggled to sleep.

Premonition

Gulls slice the air, wheeling, calling
The moon dips into a sky-blue sea
All my senses tingle
We walk the lake at sunset

The moon dips into a sky-blue sea
Clouds drift by—the trees, bare
We walk the lake at sunset
I tremble at your words

Clouds drift by—the trees, bare
You say *I'm done here*—
I tremble at your words
Your arm is the raft I cling to

You say *I'm done here*—
I thought we were your harbor
Your arm is the raft I cling to
My body quakes with loss

I thought we were your harbor—
My body quakes with loss
All my senses tingle
Gulls slice the air, wheeling, calling

A Poet Awaits Deep Brain Stimulation for Tremor

- Imagine waking from anesthesia to marvel
  at hands rendered useless with spoon,
  nail polish and pen—suddenly stilled

- See the white room, green gown, blinding
  lights, goosebumps—your shorn head,
  framed.

- Picture surgeons threading spaghetti-thin
  wires into a Tic Tac-sized target in your
  brain, sewing a battery into your chest

- Envision the machine powering poetry,
  speech, writing, gesturing temporarily
  offline

- How long until you ply words that chatter
  like chickadees, rustle like hickories
  in rain?

- Picture hands not fluttering like finches
  as you type, paper not shivering like
  a spruce in the breeze as you read

reasons to celebrate

        shadows paint Venetian blinds / across township
lawns / you stroll in darkness, then light / scrolling
        through years / easy ones that flew by / hard ones
that crawled / naked saplings reach for road like children
        begging for attention / a breeze rattles shining
yew leaves / your turbulence eased / once you
        stopped force-fitting square hopes onto round
circumstances / surrendered to reality / and looked for reasons
        to celebrate / bare branches forming iron lace
balconies against a Mardi Gras sky / God speaking
        through a cloud's brilliant mouth

A High Capacity for Suffering

And still they come, drums rolling, headlines parading the page, phones dinging at dawn, another

news cycle, *Dear God, not again*, pendulum of freedom swung too far from ancestors

who braved a tyrant, stoned a Goliath, only to become colonizers themselves—training weapons

on first nations peoples, couldn't walk a mile in their moccasins— history reloading, repeating

down the New World timeline to the present, where so many of us arm ourselves against the Other

that a plenitude of guns in pockets, purses, waistbands and nightstands makes it second nature

to react to threats, concrete or imagined—skin tint, eyefold, sexual preference, gods

worshipped, ballot boxes ticked—to elicit reptilian fear, amygdala pouring stress hormones

into our blood, fight response cascading from brain to nerves to our fingers, itching

to press triggers, ignite gunpowder, propel a projectile at a target— any veil between instinct

and action lifted, no chance for second thoughts, for clemency— lives snuffed like candles

at vigils where loved ones crumple together, and teddy bears and bouquets line fences

outside schools and synagogues and dance halls and mosques,
again and again and again and again

Still, Still, Still
> *For Mark*

West River Road snakes upward
        through a soundless panorama
                of white—maples, evergreens
        silhouetted against a cream and
pewter sky. Thick powder frosts
        rooftops—fondant on a wedding
                cake. Lights glimmer candle-like
        on porch, fence, lamppost. We
crunch uphill, boots sturdy,
        hands double-gloved, glasses
                fogged—chatting, chuckling,
        weighing the week, wordlessly
huffing, sinking into stillness—
        my favorite hour of these winter days
                with you.

holding pattern: 2020

woodsmoke pierces the air · a chainsaw growls ·
buttery dandelions stud soggy lawns · crows caw
beneath a songbird's trill · a robin dips low, orange
breast sparkling, citron beak ready · the lowering
sun stripes the road at a slant · cyclists, a lone
skateboarder fly past · tots on training wheels lap
their dad · a stroller rattles along the asphalt · we
step from homes hidden by pines, maples, hickories ·
greet each other six feet apart · minds unmoored
as the cirrus clouds above · waiting for word
on the sick · waiting for calls back to work · waiting
for Covid relief checks · waiting for grandchildren
to spill into our laps again, to kiss our wistful cheeks

Becalmed

My life a ship anchored at the pier of the pandemic,
marooned for weeks, months, a year now.
Late nights and lazy mornings,

reading, doing crosswords, walking with my partner,
eyes, ears, nose attuned to sharp,
smoke-scented winter air,

a wafer of moon dissolving in blue, clouds rippling
like sand on a tide-swept beach,
afternoon shadows

weaving a tartan blanket of branch, wire and snow.
Now a ringing chorus of peepers,
the call of a cardinal,

a squirrel's chik-chik-chik, a length of snow slumped
like a slain dragon along the road.
Grass, winter-bleached, rising

in sodden hillocks from pale, papery leaves pressed
in earth. Finally, the text arrives—Time
to schedule your Covid-19 vaccine—

breathing possibility into this quiet life, this writing
life, this fellowship of poets, friends,
family in the ether. I must weigh

my cargo carefully before I cast off into the world,
remember this calm—sailing light and trim,
venturing as far as I want to go.

Peace Amid the Pandemic

    on a thick cedar bench by the frog-muddled pond
            a sun-drunk squirrel lazily straddles a plank
    and a hummingbird hangs in the twittering calm
near the thick cedar bench by the frog-muddled pond

    no fear of the raging contagion beyond
        as a pink spider's filament silkily banks
toward the thick cedar bench by a frog-muddled pond
        where a sun-drunk squirrel lazily straddles a plank

Nothing Common About This Dandelion

With yellow petals spiky as lions' teeth • the dandelion surveys its grass terrain • unbowed by a reputation • for propagation • proud of the label *Taraxacum officinale* • less fond of *cankerwort, wild endive, yellow gowan* and *puffball* • but grateful for kids' pursed lips • to speed seeds along with wishes • waft offspring for miles on pappus parachutes • send taproots deep into earth • aerate soil, disperse nutrients • stems stretching skyward • flowers reflecting sun, moon and stars • celestial blessings • for a careless world

suitcase

love, packaged in your warm, tiny form / time
flashes past / a kid on a two-wheeler

now, you hint at distance / all I can do is watch
you soar

let your heart enfold its own / close the door gently
on the past / but leave it unlatched

stow the map of your sorrows / regret is a suitcase
best left by the roadside

resilience means surrendering to what's true /
another name for love

Thirteen Ways of Looking at a Lake
After Wallace Stevens

I
The lake wears
a mantle of molten
glass this morning.

II
This lake is vast
and blue, but clouds
shroud her green.

III
In summer, a queenly
procession of sails
takes the lake's
diamond stage.

IV
Gulls sail thermals
above the lake, dock
on her surface.

V
Jet skis plow the lake
in V formation,
mirroring geese.

VI
This lake is unmoved
by the nuisance
of motorboats.

VII
I've watched the lake's
pearlescent liquid dissolve
into atmosphere.

VIII
In winter, anyone
can see the lake's gallery
of ice sculptures
for free.

IX
Winds whip
the lake's surface
in fall, turns
it to dark chop.

X
Storms stir
water spouts
and seiches
on the lake.

XI
The lake heaves
and swells, mimicking
our anguish
and pride.

XII
Shipwrecks
are the lake's
secret.

XIII
This lake needs
no proof of the power
of her tides.

Throughline

You dream of finding words—not just any words but the right words—to conjure the 1950s, a family of 12, Vesuvian father, mother fanning embers, resentment simmering like stew on your dad's stove, cacophony of kids yelling, teasing, crying enough to drive you to Coventry Library to soar wingless to Mount Olympus, Sherwood Forest, Narnia, Oz, or pick up your pencil and draw, tracking the muse amidst chaos, banishing girlhood's errors and terrors until you can sprout wings, flee the packed nest, determined to fly—poetry your throughline connecting past to present, reflecting a checkered history of fear and hope as nimbus clouds darken the lake beneath your balcony, a resilient sun streams somewhere above.

Today: What's Beautiful
After Laura Cronk

Walking under a cobalt sky:
beautiful.

Bright cloud mimicking
an eagle bending to her chick,

a pool, warmly jacketed
for winter: beautiful.

Navy and khaki bands striping
the lake,

a colony of gulls treading
water: beautiful.

The East wind, hijacking
a shoreward tide,

Misti at our front desk,
neighbors talking weather
in the elevator: beautiful.

An electric fireplace flaming
orange and blue in our living
room,

a Diet Cherry Pepsi chilling
in the fridge: beautiful.

My desk, framed postcard
of *Nighthawks*, stained
glass lamp glowing softly
blue: beautiful.

Dogeared poetry anthology
on my nightstand,

iPad packed with library
books, fully charged:
beautiful.

The February wind whistling
through our walls:

that's not beautiful.
Neither is the blister on my heel,

or the garbage disposer making
strange sounds.

But the grey mid-Century recliner
inviting me to put my feet up,
start a poem?
Beautiful.

And my husband's silver hair
and rapt expression as he listens
to the first draft?
Gorgeous.

requiem for a nightmare

the black sky rumbles, lightning fissures the night • you're 4 years old, hurtling downhill again in a two-wheeled tumbrel • people trapped like royals en route to the Guillotine • gathering speed on a steep dirt slope • no brakes or steering • what will happen when you hit bottom? • your bones know it isn't good • the word for this is terror though you can't name it • not till you're long gone from the front-porch colonial bursting with kids • where your dad loses his job and your mom is expecting • where fear and fury coalesce and thunder into your future

Abecedarian Weather,
Cleveland, Ohio

Air quality's moderate
today · Barometer's
rising though · Cloudbursts
expected around 2 p.m. ·
Drizzle the rest of the day ·
El Nino brings wetter
winters · Fair and breezy
Monday · Gusts up to
15 miles per hour · Highs
in the mid-50s · *If you
don't like the weather,
wait a minute* · Jet
stream strong today ·
Keep your eye on the
doppler · Lake Effect
sleet and snow Tuesday
in Ashtabula · Mist
and fog make driving
hazardous · Nimbostratus
clouds massing · Overcast
skies through Wednesday ·
Partly cloudy Thursday
(or is it partly sunny)? ·
Quintessential Cleveland
weather either way ·
Rain bands cross Northeast
Ohio Friday · Small craft
advisory in effect ·
Thunderstorms likely,
possibly hail · Upper
60s and clear Saturday ·
Vortex from the North
Pole cooling things down
Sunday · Waterspouts
may form on Lake Erie ·

Xtreme · You don't see those every day · Zephyr winds are due soon, we promise (fingers crossed)

Walt Whitman, Ray Bradbury and Me
After deep brain stimulation surgery for essential tremor

I sing the body electric, for I am the electric grandmother,
factory in the future.

A battery hums inside me, calms rebel nerves bedeviling
my adolescence, adulthood—head wobbly, hands unsteady.

Now plastic and metal implants mesh with flesh to let me
       lift a latte to my lips without spilling
              line my eyelids without smudging
                     sign my name without trembling.

Today, I watch a gull flotilla bob on the lake—one soars up,
glides down like a paper airplane—my head and hands still

as the cloudless sky.

Ode to Lakewood, Ohio

Give me your fern-laden porches, your
narrow yards and buckling sidewalks,
your diner waitstaff's rainbow hair
and piercings; the vegan bakeries, crystal
shops and witch boutiques on Madison;
the same-sex couples strolling your
sidewalks. Each night, worshippers
on your solstice steps watch Lake Erie
swallow the sun like a sacrament. Now,
a head-scarved woman trains her camera
on a bouncing boy in her husband's lap,
crying *Bobo! Bobo!* As the sun melts
into the horizon, I salute your babel
of languages, your yearning to breathe free.

Erie Pantoum

Droplets plick-plick at your window,
  the heavens are leaden and grey.
Why do you love moody weather?
  Rain spills from the darkening sky.

The heavens are leaden and grey.
  Lake Erie breathes like a heaving sea.
Rain spills from the darkening sky,
  the day's gloom strangely soothing.

Lake Erie breathes like a heaving sea.
  You long for thunder and lightning,
the day's gloom strangely soothing
  as negative ions surround you.

You long for thunder and lightning.
  Wind whips the crisscrossing tides
as negative ions surround you—
  bold nimbus clouds mesmerize.

Wind whips the crisscrossing tides.
  Why do you love moody weather?
Bold nimbus clouds mesmerize.
  Droplets plick-plick at your window.

Poetry
> *after Pablo Neruda*

I wasn't ready
for you in my 20s,
though we flirted
with lyrics
by candlelight—
home & foam & sea & free,
blue ink on yellow paper,
melodies drifting
from my Gibson six-string.
Nor was I ready
in my 30s,
babies squirming
in my lap,
wails splitting
the night,
mornings an editor's chair,
minivan afternoons—
swim, dance, dinner,
homework, sleep,
repeat.
I wasn't ready,
either, in midlife—
hormones yawing,
waterfalling deadlines,
teens spoiling
for a brawl—
any urge
to shape lines & phrases
wrung dry on my PC
at work.
No, not until
I'd left 6 a.m. alarms behind
did you and I find
each other—
undaunted by aging,

you traced my life's
contours, joined
my disparate histories,
wrapped me in wonder,
stamped me
yours.

Cora McCann Liderbach, of Cleveland, Ohio, turned to writing poetry after writing and editing marketing materials for 37 years at Cleveland Clinic, an academic medical center.

Liderbach's parents met as journalists and raised ten children. Some of the poems in this volume address growing up a quiet kid in that large, noisy brood, tracing her path through the brambles of adolescence and young adulthood. Other poems illustrate the hard-won peace she found in older adulthood. Most of her poems are shot through with nature imagery, a constant source of inspiration whether she's in the city, the country or walking by Lake Erie.

At age 15, Liderbach developed a neurological condition—essential tremor—that caused her head and hands to tremble. The not-so-hidden disability interfered with fine motor skills and ended her early forays into art and music. Liderbach could still use a typewriter and computer keyboard, however, and discovered that a writing career suited her well.

In her early 70s, her tremor began to hamper Liderbach's quality of life. She underwent deep brain stimulation (DBS) surgery at Cleveland Clinic. It changed her life, allowing her to relax in the public eye. She is most grateful for the gift of DBS when taking the mic at poetry readings.

Liderbach is married with two children and two grandchildren. Her daughter, Sara, designed the cover of this book. Liderbach lives with husband Mark in Lakewood, Ohio.

Milton Keynes UK
Ingram Content Group UK Ltd.
UKHW031949281024
450365UK00008B/448